D1413084

Words

to Heal

the

Heart

Jonathon Lazear

A FIRESIDE BOOK Published by Simon & Schuster

New York London Toronto Sydney Tokyo Singapore

Remembrance of Father

FIRESIDE
Rockefeller Center
1230 Avenue of the Americas
New York, New York 10020

FIRESIDE and colophon are registered trademarks of
Simon & Schuster Inc.

Manufactured in the United States of America

DESIGNED BY BONNI LEON-BERMAN

10   9   8   7   6   5   4   3   2   1

Library of Congress Cataloging-in-Publication Data

Lazear, Jonathon.
Remembrance of father : words to heal the heart / Jonathon Lazear.
p.   cm.
"A Fireside book."
Includes bibliographical references.
1. Fathers—Death—Religious aspects—Meditations. 2.
Consolation. 3. Devotional calendars.   I. Title.
BL625.9.B47L38 1994
155.9'37'0851—dc20   94-48791
                                                              CIP

ISBN 0-684-80201-5

For

Jon M. Lazear

and

George Broad

Acknowledgments

To my wife, Wendy, and children, Michael and Ross, without whom I probably would have little insight into myself or others.

To my parents, who supplied so much love and concern.

To all those professionals and laypersons who have written brilliantly and with kindness about the subject of loss, and from whom I learned a great deal.

To my sister, Connie, and brother, Chris, who have also taught me how others let go.

To Connie Bentfield Enge, who showed how much a person can care.

With love and admiration to Beverly, Beth, Evelyn, Gregg, Amy, Leslie, Scott, and, now, Grant.

To my associates, Susie Moncur, Dennis Cass, Eric Vrooman, Cathy Groth, and Sarah Nelson Hunter.

To Tim Claussen for his wise words.

To Al Franken and John Habich, who know this loss.

And finally, to Sheila M. Curry, my wonderful editor, who knows only too well the territory this collection covers, and for her wisdom and kindness.

As always, to Marilyn Abraham. I'm truly lucky to be surrounded by such friends and professionals.

JLL
1995

Remembrance of Father

Loss

*Y*ou have to dig deep to bury your father."

—Gypsy proverb

When it happened to a friend of mine, he crawled into the darkest, deepest space inside himself—a place I did not know existed until that day. He began to feel rage. Why me? Why us? How could this happen?

He tried to impose order on his life. He clung to his calendar, a schedule, anything that created a sense of the expected that could chase away the fear of random occurrences.

Finally his rigidity began to crumble away, and months after his dad's death, he began to see that his need to control had been a self-imposed tyranny. He realized that his dad's chance car accident had given him a new kind of freedom.

Little by little he began to accept the randomness of how life begins, and, finally, how it ends.

Many feel so confused when a father dies, probably because their relationships with him were complicated. Unresolved anger, disappointment, and thoughts unspoken surface and comingle with more pure, more lucid, more positive feelings. The mixture is a strange brew, and one that we must teach ourselves to accept before we can move on.

When my uncle died, I asked my cousin what she missed most about him.

She said, "You know, I miss his silence."

I thought that was almost funny, because she'll never have to miss it again, considering he'll be silent for the rest of her days.

She went on, "It was his strength, or what we assumed was his strength. He was strong and, as I said, silent. Not really silent, of course; more like quietly intuitive. When he did speak, he almost always had something really smart and to-the-point to say. I will miss what I need to understand as that strength, and that willingness to listen. I don't know anyone else who has that trait."

His silence will be sorely missed.

Shadow and shade mix together at dawn
But by the time you catch them
Simplicity's gone
So we sort through the pieces
My friends and I
Searching through the darkness to find
The breaks in the sky.

"And the reason that she loved him
Was the reason I loved him too
And he never wondered what was
Right or wrong

"He just knew
He just knew . . ."

—*Phil Collins and*
David Crosby,
"Hero"

*T*his new reality took my friend by surprise: There is no one left who remembers him as a child. There is little tangible documentation of his early years. A few photographs, some drawings, old report cards from school. But no one to recount his early enthusiasms, his fears, his first friends, or his first words.

In a way, he feels lost. He had not realized how much of himself he would lose when he lost his father.

*I*f my father is dead, or if he was absent and cold, or if he was a tyrant, or if he abused me, or if he was wonderful but is not there for me now, then who is my father now? Where do I get those feelings of protection, authority, confidence, know-how, and wisdom that I need in order to live my life?"

—Thomas Moore,
Care of the Soul

$\mathcal{A}$s I write, I think of my own father, who is now eighty-seven. Last week I wandered among Dad's things and found myself in his library. Books. Books of all kinds are Dad's passion. Other men may have been avid armchair sports fans, or active participants, but my dad loves a great novel, a new book on science, or a brilliant autobiography.

In a way, looking through his library is like viewing his life. All of his interests, passions, and politics are displayed on his bookshelves. Maybe you can judge a man, at least in part, by what he reads and how much he reads.

I am certainly not as interested in the sciences as he is, but I will never be able to part with his Asimov, his Hawking, or his Lewis Thomas books. They will always be tangible remembrances of a richly curious man.

My father's house shines hard and bright,
It stands like a beacon calling me in the night,
Shining and calling so cold and alone
Shining across this dark highway
Where our sins lie unatoned . . ."

—Bruce Springsteen,
"My Father's House"

$\mathcal{E}$ven though Kate's dad was sick—no, terminally ill—for almost two years, she couldn't get used to the idea that she couldn't lean on him. As sick as he was, he tried so hard, especially with her kids.

She thought because denial can be so strong she lost sight of how ill he really was. She needed to hang on to the notion that he'd be there when she wanted his wise advice: "Should I get all-weather tires? What do you think of term insurance? How much should we put away for college?"

Certainly she could find the answers to these questions elsewhere. But hearing the answers from her dad made her feel secure. She trusted his opinions. They seemed thoughtful and measured. She feels like she's lost her closest, wisest, most compassionate friend.

Human beings are afraid of dying. They are always running after something: money, honor, pleasure. But if you had to die now, what would you want?"

—*Taisen Deshimara*

*I*t takes so many years
To learn that one is dead."

—*T. S. Eliot*

I am bitter.
I have been lied to.
Cheated on.
Left behind.

"Dad's gone without as much a 'good-bye.'"
Nobody told me his time was near.
I am bitter.
I am alone.

"I turned around, left town, and now he's gone.
I am angry.
We were supposed to have some final time together. Get his house and mine in order.

"But I was cheated.
Left behind.
And I'm burning mad.

"Make sure you catch him before he goes.
Your dad won't tell you because he may not know.
Keep an eye, 'cause if you're left,
You'll feel cheated, just like me."

—*Walt*

So many of us experience anger when we first encounter loss. Part of the anger has to do with a sense of abandonment.

We see our fathers as our true protectors. How can we go on without his shielding us from life's haphazard encounters?

Real or imagined, we feel like acrobats who suddenly realize they have been performing without a net. Perhaps our fathers' protection was imagined, but we feel the absence of that protection when it is suddenly gone.

There is a father-child bond regardless of how distant the father may have been during the years the child grew into adulthood.

Those of us whose fathers were self-revealing, or who were involved in daily family life, probably have deep, vivid memories of who he was and what he meant to us.

For the less fortunate, Dad may have been a shadow figure. Perhaps he died or left home before he was known to us. Those who have only mismatched puzzle pieces of memories, fragments of "who Dad was," must do their best to create an image to mourn.

How fortunate some of us are to have lasting memories of fathers that are more substantial than shadows.

The most important thing I learned on Tralfamadore was that when a person dies he only *appears* to die. He is still very much alive in the past, so it is very silly for people to cry at his funeral. All moments, past, present, and future, always have existed, always will exist. The Tralfamadorians can look at all the different moments just the way we can look at a stretch of the Rocky Mountains, for instance. They can see how permanent all the moments are, and they can look at any moment that interests them. It is just an illusion we have here on Earth that one moment follows another one, like beads on a string, and that once a moment is gone it is gone forever."

—*Kurt Vonnegut*

*I*t's strange," said a friend. "When my father died, he was living in another city, three thousand miles away. I hadn't spoken to him for a week or two, and hadn't seen him for a year. But when he died, that very night, I felt so lost, so alone."

It becomes difficult to identify the loss, to pinpoint its exact effect upon our current lives. We still get up in the morning, take a shower, get a cup of coffee, go to work, come home. The routine of our lives hasn't changed. Yet something is forever transformed.

We search for answers. If we weren't close with our father, if we spent little time with him, why do we feel such a void in our lives? Perhaps it is because we assumed he would always be there, sitting at the head of the dinner table, or behind a newspaper. If we needed to reach out to him, he would be there. When he is no longer within reach, the loss is intangible, immeasurable. It is infinite.

Our friend Amy told us that she needed to mourn silently, and that we should understand that her silence was not a rejection of our love, caring, or bereavement for her father.

Sometimes we need to look for signals—things that tell us what a survivor needs. Our best gift may be silence. The bond and support we have with dear friends sometimes do not need to be communicated with words. To be present, to be on hand *when* we are needed, may be enough.

Amy knew how we felt. We thought we understood her feelings. We did, however, have the grace not to tell her that we "knew" how she felt. When it was time for her to begin verbalizing her grief, we were there to hear her.

$\mathcal{T}$here is something about the Himalayas not possessed by the Alps, something unseen and unknown, a chain that pervades every hour spent among them, a mystery intriguing and disturbing. Confronted by them, a man loses his grasp of ordinary things, perceiving himself as immortal, an entity capable of outdistancing all change, all decay, all life, all death."

—*Frank Smythe*

When your father dies, you may try to replace his strength with your own.

You take charge. In the days that follow his death, you are grateful that you can fill your days and hours by letting others lean on you. You may lose yourself in preparing the funeral arrangements, making airline reservations for incoming family members, or writing his obituary.

Through these activities you fulfill your need to be strong, organized, and in control. Your own sense of command is a comfort to you, restoring his presence.

There will come a time, however, to take charge of your own mourning.

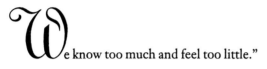

"We know too much and feel too little."

—Bertrand Russell

$\mathcal{T}$hese days families are scattered all over the country. The days of two or three generations living under one roof or even in the same neighborhood are long gone.

Carol, who lives outside of Chicago; her sisters, each living on different coasts, and her brother, up from Houston, came together when their father died. Their lives had dispersed them not only geographically but emotionally as well.

The first two days after they gathered in Columbus it was as if four strangers had arrived to mourn the loss of a man who had been a different person for each one of them.

During the time they spent together, they traded wonderful, important, heartfelt stories of their father. No longer were they strangers; never were they closer, nor had they ever felt more compassion for one another, than at their father's funeral.

$\mathcal{P}$eople sleep, and when they die they wake."

—*Muhammad*

Grief

W e must face what we fear; that is the case of the core of the restoration of health."

—*Max Lerner*

*B*eware of undertaking too much at the start. Be content with quite a little. Allow for accidents. Allow for human nature, especially your own."

—*Arnold Bennett*

$\mathcal{T}$he numbness of disbelief soon enough turns into the isolation of grief. Your relationship with your father is unique. Your sister or brother or mother knew him, but not in the same way that you knew him.

While it is good to honor the uniqueness of your relationship with your father, it is also important to grieve with others. Loss is a frightening, isolating, and cold reality. It may help if your family pulls together now, for strength, solidarity, and to share the commonality of bereavement.

*T*he children of a friend of ours who died seemed to feel responsible for their father's death. Young children often feel responsible for loss, divorce, illness, and other family traumas.

It was very important for David's wife to explain to their children that his death had nothing to do with them. Moreover, it was equally important for the children to see and hear their mother's grief. She needed them to know how profound was her loss. When she opened up to them, the children shared their loss with her as well. Sharing grief was the beginning of healing.

Our friend Elaine told us that she was so sorry not to have been at her father's side when he died.

She tried desperately to get to the hospital, but by the time she arrived the priest had already delivered last rites and her father was dead.

"Dad should not have been alone. I know that death is a singular and final act, but I still believe that had I been there it may have made a difference to him . . . or to both of us."

Guilt is certainly part of the grief process. But we must let it pass, remembering that Dad would not want to have it burden us for the rest of our days.

*L*et us no more contend, nor blame
Each other, blam'd enough elsewhere, but strive
In offices of love, how we may lighten
Each other's burden, in our share of woe."

—*John Milton*,
Paradise Lost

*G*rief counselors tell us there are phases that everyone who mourns must pass through. They remind us that we may not progress through them one by one, and that there may be days when we take a few steps back. Forcing oneself through them too quickly may lead to a false sense of well-being. Everyone must allow grief to follow the course that is right for him or her. Some need to stave off the reality of loss by remaining in denial before moving on. Others may feel that solitary mourning is right for them. How we grieve is as individual as who we are.

$\mathcal{E}$ach child in a family grieves for his or her father in a different way. Although they share the loss, they have seen his life in their own terms. They have had a different relationship with him.

Perhaps our illusions of who and what our fathers have been are as strong as the realities of their lives. Because our fathers are unique to each of us, our grief and our loss are unique, too.

Nothing can make up for the absence of someone whom we love, and it would be wrong to find a substitute. We must simply hold out and see it through. That sounds very hard at first, but at the same time it is a great consolation. For the gap, as long as it remains unfilled, preserves the bonds between us . . . The dearer and richer our memories, the more difficult the separation.

"But gratitude changes the pangs of memory into tranquil joy. The beauties of the past are borne, not as a thorn in the flesh, but as a precious gift in themselves . . . In this way the past gives us lasting joy and strength."

—*Dietrich Bonhoeffer*

Our friend Diane enjoyed the sense of control she had had over life. Her father's death sent her into a tailspin of depression. Embarrassed by her inability to regain her strong sense of self, she began to hide even from her mother, who needed her at the time.

Diane finally acknowledged her depression. No doubt it was due to the unresolved issues she had with her father. She felt anger and disappointment, and she had questions that would probably go unanswered.

Diane had to sort through her loss to find the salvageable, important memories for her to hold on to. She fought hard against the depression, consulted a wonderful therapist, and survived.

Her father would have been proud.

Steve had been given the name of a professional grief counselor. He was reluctant to attend a meeting because he didn't trust the group process. It seemed too "Oprah," too open, too exhibitionistic.

After his second meeting with a group of adults, all of whom had recently lost a parent, he began to feel strength and genuine support from these people.

Not one to share his feelings easily, it was difficult for him to talk at first. But soon he realized that these people had experienced the trauma of loss, and they had much in common.

He finally realized that the grief process need not be borne privately. It can help to have the support of peers, especially those who have suffered a similar loss.

$\mathcal{C}$ompare your griefs with those of other men and they will seem less."

—*Spanish proverb*

$\mathcal{D}$on't waste your time trying to control the uncontrollable . . . solve the problems you can solve with the wisdom you have gained from both your victories and your defeats. . . ."

—David Mahoney

Sometimes the grieving process is like running a marathon.

The day starts out sunny. You do your stretches and your warm-ups, and you start out your run with great anticipation and positive expectation.

The clouds roll in and the rain comes up, not at your back, but directly in your face. Your breathing pattern changes, and, moving along through the storm of emotions, muscles aching, you take comfort in knowing your race for the day is nearly over, and you'll have made yourself that much stronger by getting through it.

When the rain gives way to sunshine and the pavement dries, you know you can ride out another storm—which may come with the dawn.

I thought I could describe a state; make a map of sorrow. Sorrow however turns out to be not a state but a process."

—*C. S. Lewis*

*Y*ou need to remember, but it hurts to remember. This is the paradox of loss.

If you think back to the times when he was there for you, you invariably remember the times he was not. If you summon a warm, private memory from your youth, you are suddenly sad that you did not spend more time with him as an adult. If you reflect on his face as a younger man, warm and tanned by his active lifestyle, you remember how sad he looked right before he died, hunched over in his favorite chair, struggling to hear you speak to him. Every positive, nourishing thought is accompanied by an equally negative one.

You can be dragged down by this painful process of remembering. But the memories—all of them—must be allowed to come to the surface. You cannot hold them back.

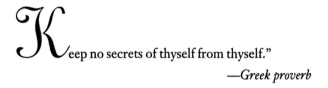

$\mathcal{K}$eep no secrets of thyself from thyself."

—*Greek proverb*

$\mathcal{M}$y cousin somewhat sheepishly admitted something that she's done for the past year since my uncle died.

She's been writing him letters. Obviously she doesn't send them anywhere. She simply composes notes to him, whenever she feels the urge, telling him things she was never able to say while he was alive, giving him advice, recalling a story from the past, getting him caught up with the doings of his two grandchildren and herself.

She told me this helps her enormously. She said it helps her to grieve quietly, but expressively. It is a wonderful gift that she's giving herself.

*A*s someone who was nearly famous for avoiding problems, Leslie was expected to sidestep any grief when her father died last year.

But she surprised all of us. She met her grief head-on. Somehow she knew that she could survive his loss by giving in to it, admitting it, going with it. She was remarkable. She began keeping a journal and going to a grief counselor, and she wasn't afraid to talk about how she felt.

Her insights were superb. Because she had so fully accepted her father during his life, his strengths *and* his weaknesses, she was far more able to accept his death. She had never put him on a pedestal during his life. She accepted him as he was. Her loss revealed a side of her that we'd never seen.

Moreover, she began to talk about her father more and more. By listening to her we learned a great deal about him and about Leslie, too.

A friend and client mentioned to me that he was using meditation to help him through his grief. He told me that he had come from a family that was extravagant—in fact, too extravagant—in showing their emotions. He told me that he couldn't stand to visit them after his father died because each member of his family attempted to "outmourn" the next, as though they were participating in an emotional Olympics.

He decided that it was best for him to retreat. He made the decision to work out the conflicts and sadness he felt by turning within, and mourning privately.

Months later, he said that he thought he'd made a good choice. "Besides," he told me, "I've kept up my daily meditation, and it's helped ease my life's tensions, not just helped me cope with Dad's death."

Strength is a capacity for endurance. One of the dividends of suffering is the universal discovery that we possess a strength within us we never knew we had. Navigating through a difficult episode not only shows us that inner strength is there but convinces us it will always be there to serve us in the future. Overcoming gives us an assurance of personal confidence and value that far exceeds what we thought we possessed before our struggles began."

—Dennis Wholey

$\mathcal{T}$om had trouble moving through mourning.

"After a while—it was three or four months, I guess—I realized that I was stuck in a rut, or couldn't get past a certain part of my grief."

Recognizing that he was stuck helped him get beyond that point of bereavement: "I wasn't being productive, and my grief or anger or denial, wasn't productive, either. I felt, after I acknowledged this, like a fog lifted.

"Sure, I was still sad that Dad had died, especially at such a young age. But I really do believe that he wouldn't want me to spend any more time harboring my sorrow and rejecting those around me. I feel a certain resolution and a new sense of freedom."

*F*ace grief without any expectation of miraculous healing, but with the knowledge that if we are courageous and resolute we can live as our loved ones would wish us to live, not empty, morose, self-centered, and self-pitying, but as brave and undismayed servants of the greater life . . ."

—*Joshua Loth Liebman*

*I*t's important to trust yourself during bereavement.

I know of a friend who took off with his wife and kids on a planned vacation only ten days after his Dad died.

It turned out to be a very important part of his healing. He got away from the familiar surroundings of his father's business and house, where he certainly would have been immersed in pain. He separated himself from the constant reminders of his father.

His vacation was not as bright or carefree as it normally would have been. (After all, his grief could not be left behind.) But the separation came at a very good time, and it helped him enormously. He knew in his heart that it was the right thing to do.

$\mathcal{I}$ do not feel that I'm betraying him for laughing, for loving, for becoming whole again.

"It is because of him that I've come through the grief as a person stronger, more courageous, and less superficial than ever before.

"It is because of his wit, his warmth, his intelligence, and his unique mind that I can move forward, looking back in love.

"It is because of him that my children had a strong memory of a grandfather who was very much involved in their world.

"It is because of him that I now can look back with the warm thoughts and tender feelings of a life that was a gift to me."

—Anonymous

$\mathcal{Y}$et in the agony of my spirit in surrendering such a treasure I feel a thousand times richer than if I had never possessed it."

—*William Wordsworth*

$\mathcal{A}$ dying man needs to die as a sleepy man needs to sleep, and there comes a time when it is wrong, as well as useless, to resist."

—*Stewart Alsop*

*T*here are two experiences in life that defy description.

The first is birth. Seeing my two sons being born filled me with a joy and reverence for life that cannot be put into words.

The other, to be sure, is somber, sad, and breathtaking. The final separation, accompanied by the feeling of uselessness, of wanting desperately to stop the inevitable; watching the life ebb from someone so dear and so important is the second most astonishing time in life.

$\mathcal{M}$y Dad left the house every morning and always seemed glad to see everyone at night.

"He opened the jar of pickles when no one else could.

"He was the only one in the house who wasn't afraid to go into the basement by himself.

"He cut himself shaving, but no one kissed it or got excited about it.

"He signed all my report cards. He put me to bed early. He took lots of pictures, but was never in them.

"I was afraid of everyone else's father, but not my own. Once I made him tea. It was only sugar water, but he sat on a small chair and said it was delicious. He looked very uncomfortable.

"Whenever I played house, the mother doll had a lot to do. I never knew what to do with the daddy doll, so I had him say, 'I'm going off to work now' and threw him under the bed.

"When I was nine years old, my father didn't get up one morning and go to work. He went to the hospital and died the next day.

"I went to my room and felt under the bed for the father doll. When I found him, I dusted him off and put him on my bed.

"He never did anything. I didn't know his leaving would hurt so much.

"I still don't know why."

—*Erma Bombeck*

$\mathcal{T}$he father is the most powerful incarnation of the arche-typal masculine."

—*Carl Jung*

Some months after his father died, John said, "I'm lucky, because his shoe size is identical to mine. I can wear all of his work boots." John is a newspaper editor, a classically trained pianist, and a writer—he's never needed a pair of work boots.

"You know what else?" he asked. "I also now have a full set of wrenches, screwdrivers, pliers, and hammers!"

If John ever used a hammer, it was to hang a piece of art. He has not been known to be handy—he's no Mr. Fix-It. But part of John's grief was to keep those things his father used. It is also a way for him to celebrate and maintain a connection with his father. He needed to salvage those things that were tangible relics of his father's life. He seemed almost proud of those newfound tools. "I really think I'll use them . . . someday."

*D*an's dad was chronically ill. He had diabetes for over a decade. Those first years with the illness were uncertain—would he get better? Would he lose his eyesight? Were his kidneys going to fail?

Each year that went by and Dan's father beat the odds, Dan felt what so many children who have parents with long-term illness feel: relief because maybe they've beaten it—at least for now. This reprieve involves bargaining for time; surely they'll find a new medicine, some new treatment. A miracle will occur. After all, millions of people live long lives with diabetes.

When Dan's father died of complications of diabetes, Dan looked back and understood how long he had been attempting to control something he had no power over. Dan's grief was, in some ways, less severe than that of others who have lost their fathers. Even though Dan was hoping for his dad's recovery, he knew that death was coming, it was just taking its time.

$\mathcal{L}$ive riotously. It is foolish to sit around waiting for the collector when the collector may be late. And if . . . the New Testament, Buddha, and the Koran are right, it may not be over even then. You'll either be with your pals in paradise or you won't feel a thing."

—*David Brown*

$\mathcal{I}$ don't think, no matter what I did or what I said," my friend Eric told me, "that I ever really demonstrated my love for my father. Now I look back and I feel guilty for not being there when my stepmother died. Dad was all alone. I could have helped." Now that his father was gone, Eric wishes he could have told him he was sorry for not being supportive.

Eric's feelings of guilt and his anxiety about his not "being there" for his father are common. We must, though, get past the regret. It is far better to remember those times when you were there for your father. Remember the times when your love and support were felt, noted, and deeply appreciated.

$\mathcal{A}$nne blamed her father's doctor for not being able to save him. She had pinned all her hopes on the professional's authority and notoriety. She saw him as a miracle worker who didn't come through with a miracle.

Anne needed to blame someone for the devastation that she felt. So many of us become angry at the reality of loss. It may be irrational—Anne's father had been in a steady decline for more than a year—but she held fast to what she wanted her father's specialist to do.

Now Anne knows her father could not be saved, and she is at peace with her loss.

*E*veryone of us gladly turns away from his problems; if possible they must not be mentioned, or better still their experience is denied. We wish to make our lives simple, certain and smooth. And for that reason problems are taboo. The artful denial of a problem will not produce conviction; on the contrary, a wider and higher consciousness is called for to give us the certainty and clarity we need."

—Carl Jung

$\mathcal{M}$y father has season tickets to all the Twins games," my friend Shelby told me. "We go every chance we get. He gets such a kick out of my kids and their interest in the game."

The jealousy I felt at that moment was like a punch in the stomach. It was a clear message: Nothing like that will happen to us again. He'll no longer take pride in my kids' accomplishments, we won't gather regularly for any event, and I'm feeling very sorry for myself, and for my family.

Later on I let the anger and jealousy subside. It's really wonderful Shelby has that time with his father and children. When his father dies, he'll have those memories to keep with him.

$\mathcal{I}$ thought that I had supplied only marginal support for my friend Al during his dad's last days and subsequent death.

Some time ago, in an uncharacteristic moment of reflection, Al told me I was wrong. He said that just my being around, and in touch with him during those last days, and later by phone, meant a great deal to him. He went on to say that my "normal" presence in his life gave him some semblance of normalcy during a time of extreme emotional upset. He said, "All that time I was trying to say good-bye to Dad, I knew I could always say hello to you."

I have rarely, if ever, felt better about being there for a friend.

$\mathcal{T}$he missing father is not your or my personal father. He is the absent father in our culture, the viable senex who provides not daily bread but spirit through meaning and order. The missing father is the dead God who offered a focus for spiritual things."

—*James Hillman*

*I*n the evening of life, we will be judged on love alone."

—*St. John of the Cross*

$\mathcal{S}$ometimes we are faced with the question, Is my father determined to live? And if he isn't, is it because he has not felt the power of our love?

Why can't we fix this? Why can't we get the right doctor? Why didn't he go for the tests earlier? When did he *really* begin to feel bad?

Was he being "strong" for us? Was this the ultimate act of caring, of being selfless?

Facing the end of his days and trying to put a good face on it is the cruelest thing that can happen to any of us.

At some point, we want to be wanted. We want our fathers and mothers to *need us*. When they are in denial and don't reach out to us, it can be a harsh experience. When a parent dies, we can be angry because they did not let us help them through this passage.

But, of course, we forgive. But we never forget.

We need to be reminded that there is nothing morbid about honestly confronting the fact of life's end, and preparing for it so that we may go gracefully and peacefully . . . The fact is, we cannot truly face life until we have learned to face the fact that it will be taken away from us."

—Billy Graham

$\mathcal{M}$y friend Refna told me that she wanted to leave her Dad's apartment totally intact after he died. For more than seven months she continued to pay the rent, water the plants, and take in the mail and the newspaper.

I knew she was in great pain, but she was also in great denial.

Refna's refusal to accept her father's death, and the way in which she did her best to maintain the appearance that he was living were extreme. When she was finally confronted by the economic reality that she simply could not continue to pay for his apartment, she broke down.

It was inevitable that reality would intercede. I'm sorry that she felt she needed to work so hard to fend off his loss for so long and went to such great lengths to preserve the illusion of her father's presence in her life.

I do believe, though, that she did resolve many long-standing issues she had with him—maybe, to some extent, because she allowed herself to be immersed in his home and his belongings.

When eating bamboo sprouts, remember the men who planted them."

—*Chinese proverb*

*O*ur friend Stephanie had been taking care of her father, who lived with her and her two children for several years. Stephanie was divorced when her second daughter was still a baby.

Stephanie was amazing. She held down her job, took care of the kids, and became her father's night nurse when his health went downhill. She never had any time for herself, never went on vacation, never indulged in any hobby or outside activity. She was the essence of control.

After her father died, she became increasingly depressed. For so long, order and responsibility had been her means of holding on to and keeping a grip on her world. Without being in total control, and occupied by taking charge, she *had* no life.

It took over a year for her to come to grips with her dad's death. Once she did, it was a life-saving release for her. Throughout her dad's illness she was in denial, but denial enabled her to be the strongest one around. Now she's learned that it's time for her to indulge herself in *her* life.

$\mathcal{T}$he ancient intuition that all matter, all "reality" is energy, that all phenomena, including time and space, are mere crystallizations of mind, is an idea with which few physicists have quarreled since the theory of relativity first called into question the separate identities of energy and matter. Today, most scientists would agree with the ancient Hindus that nothing exists or is destroyed, things merely change shape or form; that matter is insubstantial in origin, a temporary aggregate of the pervasive energy that animates the electron."

—Peter Matthiessen

$\mathcal{I}$ had shunned organized religion all my life. To me, it seemed confining, rigorous, and detached from the human experience.

Only after my father's death did I begin to understand not only what the church or synagogue can provide; only then did I begin to think about what's beyond.

When poet Langston Hughes asks, "What happens to a dream deferred?" he wants to know how or if the power of will, the dream, and the soul and spirit just disappears or does it explode?

Where does the energy that is much in evidence during a person's life go?

I am beginning to think that the souls of our loved ones are still out there. Their energies remain with us—if we let them in.

$\mathcal{G}$od, grant me the serenity

To accept the things I cannot change;

Courage to change the things I can;

And the wisdom to know the difference."

—Reinhold Niebuhr

Moving On

It does not matter how slowly you go so long as you do not stop."

—*Confucius*

*I*f a father dies when his children are very young, his influence lives on and is often exaggerated through images of him that become fantasy. Fathers are often idealized, and the more that happens, says Betty Carter, "The more negativity may be directed toward the mother, who is, after all, 'merely human.'"

Because a father who has died is so idealized, he is, as Carter says, "flash-frozen in perfection."

Because most of us want desperately to remember our fathers in the best light possible, we often create a father figure that is mythical or inaccurate at best, which doesn't reflect who he really was.

As time goes on, little by little his true image can be recollected. Time helps to separate what was real from what was ideal.

*M*emories can help us heal.

Some say the first year is the hardest, and that things begin to get better after that. Birthdays and holidays are hard to get through, and one wonders what Dad would have thought of how handsome and talented the kids have become and how proud he would have been of their science project, their photography, or their baseball games. We resist the urge to pick up the phone to tell him about our raise; we stop ourselves from clipping and sending him that newspaper article he would have liked.

It may be good to fantasize about those things. Maybe it's healthy to imagine that he's there for graduation or for his granddaughter's wedding. Just imagine how he would have felt, and how bright his smile would have been.

ear Jonathon,

I tried so hard to answer your letter promptly, but everything I wrote (or tried to write) was just a shadow of how I really felt.

You know Dad died in '92, just as I was moving back from France. He never let on how he was really doing. I knew he was sick, but he (and no one else) never let on about how sick he really was.

So when I got back to Columbus, anticipating his strong arms to hug me, welcoming me back home, I was truly horrified by who and what had become of him, after only eight months of my being away.

It's taken me so long to sort out these feelings. Part of me was so damned angry that I was "spared" the truth of how gravely ill he was. Part of me denied it, too. I just couldn't get used to seeing the man who meant more to me than any other person in the world so weak, so needy, and, finally, so dishonest.

In the name of protecting me, he didn't allow me to acclimate myself to his imminent passing.

I first thought, "What have I done to make him distrust my emotions, my love, my dedication, to him?" It's taken me all this time to really understand that it was his final act of protection, love, and selflessness that made him hide the truth of his final days. I will never forget that final kindness. I do not think I have the kind of strength he showed me while he hid the pain, anguish, and unfettered love he had for me. I only hope I can be unselfish in my pain for those I love when it is my time.

Do take care.

Carol

$\mathcal{F}$letch, Dad's hunting dog, planted himself at the foot of Father's bed. This was not his usual place to sleep. Fletch was a hunting dog, and, while loyal and friendly, he was very independent. But toward the end of Dad's life, Fletch became ever more loyal. Dad wasn't available for hunting, fetching, running, or active companionship, but Fletch somehow knew that Dad needed him.

There are so many "friendly dog" stories around. This one astounded all of us. Fletch exhibited similar symptoms of my father's illness: on-again, off-again sleep, mood swings, a need for privacy.

His behavior did truly mirror almost all of Dad's behavior. Some mornings we looked to Fletch to tell us how Dad was feeling, and what to expect for the day.

One of my earliest memories is that of my father pushing me in the swing in the backyard of our house. I felt like I was going to fly right up into the trees. I was exhilarated, a little frightened, and my heart was racing. I felt so close to him then. It's probably my first memory of being vulnerable but under his protection. I knew he would not endanger me. He knew just how hard to push, and how high I should go.

Pushing my youngest in his swing some thirty years later, hearing him squeal with laughter, repeating over and over, "Oh, Dad, oh, Dad," I remember how small my world was when I was his age, and how I feel now, a generation later, repeating this simple act of love and trust with my own son. He must feel in a safe harbor. I know I do.

*E*lisabeth Kübler-Ross offers us predictable stages of the dying and death process: denial, anger, bargaining, depression, and acceptance. That these stages apply also to major adversity seems possible, although debatable. What appears true, however, is that in confronting adversity, there are common denominators for overcoming hardship: faith, hope, attitude, acceptance, and action.

"While we are truly powerless in many situations, our future is more in our hands than we often believe. Self-pity and victimization get us nowhere. Decision-making, initiative, and behavior—all components of action—propel us toward personal victories in difficult times.

"Activity, which takes us out of ourselves, creates interaction with others, distracts us from an upset, and moves us toward our goal of recovery. Traumatic situations present challenges that require focus, goal setting, risk, and effort. Meeting those challenges produces the good feelings of high self-esteem, the satisfaction of accomplishment, and options for the future."

—*Dennis Wholey*,
When the Worst
That Can Happen
Already Has

*G*rowing up in a home where Dad may be the great provider but is otherwise invisible does not provide a child with the impetus to get to know his father.

After he is gone it is too late. You must piece together from the shards of his past a replica of this man. What kind of music did he like? What authors? What sports? Why?

So much of a man's life is kept private that one sometimes needs to grieve not just for what has been lost, but for what has been undiscovered. When the man who provided for you is gone and you never really knew him as a person, you face a double tragedy.

Some years ago, I was helping my father move from the big family house to a manageable apartment and elder care facility.

While packing, I came across a small box tied with what looked like an ancient pink ribbon. Inside were dozens of letters written by my father to my mother during the war. He traveled a great deal, although he was not abroad, and his letters were tender, funny, full of news, and long. He wrote almost daily to her, and I was privileged to see a side of him I had never known before.

I never told him I read those letters. It was, after all, a somewhat dishonest thing to do. But I am so glad I did, because I caught a glimpse of a man who had disappeared. And it helped me see the man who was with me now in a new light.

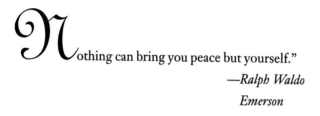othing can bring you peace but yourself."

—*Ralph Waldo*
Emerson

*D*uring one of my father's hospital stays, it seemed he might not live through the night. His doctor mistakenly reported that he had cancer of the pancreas, which is always fast and fatal. We had just begun to allow what we thought was fact to sink in.

I sat up with him most of the night. Our conversation, although it was halting and emotional, was, in a way, sacred.

My father did not die that night. But he and I were able to begin to prepare for the eventuality of his death.

Even though I was able to be with him, I never felt so alone. I felt my protector was about to vanish, and there was absolutely nothing I could do to stop it.

*I*n laying myself down like ash after the flame
Have I surrendered?
No, I am sleeping and despite night's power
Learning like a child that I shall awake."

—*Paul Eluard*

I have so many memories.

I remember the night I brought the car home too late and, in typical teenage fashion, waited for the sermon.

He did not give it. He took the keys from my outstretched hand, gave me a gentle smile, said, "Good night, son," and headed toward his room.

I stared after him for a long time, wondering why he hadn't given me the expected tirade of words. I felt almost cheated out of a scolding.

But now, years later, I think I'm on to him. I must try this with my own son someday.

$\mathcal{S}$ome years before he died, two women from the local hospice came to visit my dad.

We thought he had less than two months to live. He was remarkably clear about it. The two women who came to the house were enormously kind and sympathetic, but direct.

He welcomed them in as though they'd come to assess the house for repainting. Somehow, he seemed to find comfort in knowing that the end was near.

As it turned out, he lived many more years. But I have never forgotten how stalwart, how gentlemanly, and with how much grace he allowed them into what he thought were his last days.

$\mathcal{I}$f there's one thing I'm grateful for, it's that I kept every single letter that my father ever sent me. From the time I was twelve years old, at sleepaway camp, until very recently—I've kept every note, every newspaper clipping, everything that he sent to me.

I may never go back and read everything. I do take comfort in the fact that I can if I want to. He had such a marvelous sense of humor. Of course, earlier in his correspondence were warnings of all kinds—don't get too serious about one girl or another, keep your nose to the grindstone. He also included congratulations (on making the dean's list) and all the news from home—a new birdfeeder, a warmer house for the dog, how Mother was making progress after her stroke.

These letters form a verbal map of our life together and apart. They echo part of the life of a man I shall miss the rest of my days.

*I*t's a risk to attempt new beginnings. Yet the greater risk is for you to risk nothing. For there will be no further possibilities of learning and changing, of traveling upon the journey of life. You were strong to hold on. You will be stronger to go forward to new beginnings."

—*Rabbi Dr. Earl Grollman*, Time Remembered: A Journal for Survivors

$\mathcal{M}$any people seem to be keeping journals or diaries these days. It's something I tried to maintain faithfully a couple of times, but I never kept up with it daily.

I think, looking back, that one of the best, most helpful, and healthy things I did during those early days of mourning was to record daily, sometimes twice or three times a day, my thoughts, especially those about my father.

As I look back and reread some of the passages, I am pleased to discover I have recorded some wonderful memories of my father—stories, quotes, and little vignettes that may have been lost to time and failing memory.

*T*here can be no resolution of mourning and loss until you put the question of 'Why?' behind . . . [Instead ask], 'How do I survive and find courage? How can I take this life-shattering trauma and make it a basis for growing?'"

—*Mrs. A. J. Levinson*
and Harold S.
Kushner

*I*t took us months after Dad died to look at the old photo albums and the videotapes we had recorded at Christmas, birthdays, and other occasions.

One day we decided that we missed him so much that we thought it would be great to spend the day with him. I didn't know I had the courage to do this, but it turned out wonderfully.

There he was, Christmas Eve, helping the kids hang their stockings, singing the whole time. Another video showed him at our youngest son's fourth birthday—hugging him, laughing, and tossing balloons over his head. Then we went to the photo album—the ones with Mom; my sister and brother as kids; our first train trip to Chicago; with our grandparents in Florida.

It was a magical day. I am so glad I faced up to celebrating his life, not mourning it. Yes, all of us miss him. But we rectified our love and our memories of him that day.

*T*his didn't happen all of a sudden, but about a month after the first anniversary of Dad's death, I started to take account of what I *did* have, the people in my life who I value tremendously, and I thought, 'Maybe this is the way the first year of bereavement ends,' maybe re-entering the world of *my* family and of my children, taking stock in what I have that is sacred to me, and truly reveling in that, maybe I've passed the point of obsession, and now can go on with memories intact, but no longer overloaded with the burden of Dad's passing."

—*B. Taylor*

*M*y father, folding toward the earth again, plays his harmonica and waves his white handkerchief as I drive off over the hills to reclaim my life.

"Each time, I am sure it's the last, but it's been this way now for twenty-five years: my father waving and playing 'Auf Wiedersehen,' growing thin and blue as a late-summer iris, while I who have the heart for love but not the voice for it, disappear into the day, wiping the salt from my cheeks and thinking of women. There is no frenzy like the frenzy of his happiness, and frenzy, I know now, is never happiness: only the loud, belated cacophony of a lost soul having its last dance before it sleeps forever.

"The truth, which always hurts, hurts now—I have always wanted another father: *one who would sit quietly beneath the moonlight, and in the clean, quiet emanation of some essential manhood, speak to me of what, a kind man myself, I wanted to hear.*

"*But this is not a poem about self-pity: As I drive off, a deep masculine quiet rises, of its own accord, from beneath my shoes. I turn to* watch my father's white handkerchief flutter, like an old Hasid's prayer shawl, among the dark clouds and the trees. I disappear into the clean, quiet resonance of my own life. To live, *dear father, is to forgive.*

And I forgive."

—Michael Blumenthal,
"Waving Good-bye
to My Father"

*F*orgive, son; men are men, they needs must err."

—*Euripides*

I have always been the stalwart, strong, silent, nonexpressive kind of guy," my friend Dennis told me.

"But when my father died, and he died suddenly, I just couldn't keep up the act of being the pillar of emotional stability. I lost interest in my job, my mind often wandered, I had fits of dark depression, and I felt so lonely.

"In the weirdest kind of paradox, though, his death and my subsequent emotional roller-coaster ride helped me rid myself of the inflexibility I had always prided myself on. My father's death gave me the chance to become a full person. In a way, I look at his passing as a gift. I feel like a fully realized person now, and I'm grateful for it."

*Y*ou say good-bye to your father only to say hello to a new spirit in yourself.

Forced to take a character inventory, you make a startling discovery: That which is good and made you strong and helped you "get through" is the same character you derived from your father.

In so many ways, you can bring to the world some of the same ethics, interests, and values that your father bequeathed you. In those ways he lives on. Perhaps some of the best, most desirable components of his personality and talents can, through your life and deeds, stay alive. In this way you can celebrate what he has passed down to you, keeping it alive long after you've said good-bye.

*O*ur search for Father, we discover, is unending. Plato said, 'The life which is unexamined is not worth living.' The same is true of the father-child relationship. If we never bothered to analyze our father's impact on our lives, now is the time to start. If we thought we knew him and what impact he had—and still has—on our lives, it's time to look again. . . It is not enough for us to say we never really knew him, and let it go at that. For in fathoming him, we can at last fathom ourselves."

> —*Christopher P.*
> *Anderson,* Father:
> The Figure and the
> Force

Books to help you make the journey:

Anderson, Christopher P. *Father: The Figure and the Force.* New York: Warner Books, 1981.

Beattie, Melody. *A Reason to Live.* Chicago: Tyndale House, 1992.

Callanon, Maggie and Patricia Kelley. *Final Gifts: Understanding the Special Awareness, Needs, and Communication of the Dying.* New York: Poseidon Press, 1992.

Coughlin, Ruth Pollock. *Grieving: A Love Story.* New York: Random House, 1993.

Kramer, Herbert and Kay. *Conversations at Midnight: Coming to Terms with Dying and Death.* New York: William Morrow, 1993.

Levang, Elizabeth, Ph.D. and Sherokee Ilse. *Remembering with Love: Messages of Hope for the First Year of Grieving and Beyond.* Minneapolis: Deaconess Press, 1992.

O'Connor, Nancy, Ph.D. *Letting Go with Love: The Grieving Process.* New York: Bantam Books, 1984.

Scull, Charles S. (editor). *Fathers, Sons and Daughters.* Los
    Angeles: Jeremy P. Tarcher, 1992.

Standacher, Carol. *Men and Grief.* Oakland, CA: New Harbin-
    ger Publications, 1991.

Wholey, Dennis. *When the Worst That Can Happen Already Has:
    Conquering Life's Most Difficult Times.* New York: Hyper-
    ion Books, 1992.

Printed in the United States
68451LVS00001B/100